My Year In Therapy

Daniel McGowan

BookLeaf Publishing
India | USA | UK

Presentation by *BookLeaf Publishing*

Web: www.bookleafpub.com

E-mail: info@bookleafpub.com

ISBN: 978-93-5744-387-6

First edition 2022

DEDICATION

For my big sister who has long acted as my moral compass and friend.

Here's to daring to be different big sister.

ACKNOWLEDGEMENT

To my therapist who listened with kindness and care. Who went on a journey with me and helped me learn to forgive and believe in myself again.

To my family who raised me to be the man that I am today. Who taught me right from wrong and to always choose to be kind.

To the friends that became like family. Whose support, humor and friendship helped me find my way back.

To the girl that has got me smiling. Who I don't think I would have ever finished writing this without her support and belief in me.

Thank you. You are all what got me here.

PREFACE

I kind of fell into therapy this time.

I had been to therapy before, just after my sister passed. It was grief counseling and it was really helpful. It was also a great way for me to talk about and remember my sister.

This time around was different. I had been living in London for just over a year, something my big sister and I dreamed about doing together.

In a year of lockdowns, relationship breakdowns and so much change, I sought out therapy again. It was at a time where I felt like I had nowhere to turn to and I felt lost physically and mentally. Honestly, I can't really remember ever feeling worse.

Therapy, it was uncomfortable at first, learning to speak my truth. To open up about my past trauma and feel every painful emotion again. I had locked my trauma away for a really long time, and I didn't ever dare think to confront it. It was time to change.

Speaking openly to a professional, seeking out therapy - it turned out to be the best thing I ever did. I spoke about the impact of the past year. I spoke about the impact of my last 29 years. I spoke painful truths and I was more vulnerable then I have ever been.

But somewhere in amongst all that talking I had learnt to find comfort and peace in my journey. It had been long and it had been immeasurably painful, but I had survived whatever came my way. It took patience, fierce determination and courage to confront and push the demons away, but with time I discovered the true meaning of healing and peace.

It is my hope that by being open about my mental health journey in my writing that I encourage others to seek out help. That it acts as a reminder to others that they aren't alone in what they're feeling. That there is help out there for them too.

Please know that you are never alone. It gets better, I promise.

Therapy: A Journey

Somewhere in all the darkness you lost yourself and the person you are. You danced with anxiety and fear and held onto anything that brought you joy, even when that joy was temporary.

It took time, and it will still take time but you found yourself. It was no longer through the eyes of another or through what others thought of you, but finally, how you saw yourself. You learnt to stand tall even when it meant standing alone and found confidence, trust and security in the person you are. You woke up from the nightmare and remembered your true value.

You learnt that even when your world fell apart and felt as though a vase called your life fell to the floor and crashed into a thousand pieces, that there was beauty in being broken. You learnt to pick those pieces up one by one, as vulnerable and fragile as they were and started to piece things back together.

And all you ever really wanted was what used to be, who you used to be. But you also learned that the puzzle didn't have to be put back together and resemble what it once was. You discovered that you had to make a whole new puzzle entirely. A new puzzle full of hope, of joy, and love and you discovered a whole new lease on life called healing and peace.

You found yourself and you got back to enjoying the journey of life. You learnt that it doesn't have to consume you and that it doesn't have to change who you are. And when finally you chose yourself you learnt that neither fire nor flood could wipe you away, because you learnt to shine brighter every single day.

Goal Setting

1. Understanding the impact of the last year and how it has affected my confidence and who I am

2. Getting back to enjoying the journey of life

3. Understanding why I feel anxious and vulnerable with relationships.

My Promise

Big sister, this is my promise

I'll hold dad's hand and I'll take mum's heart,
Our younger sister and me we won't grow apart
We will take you with us wherever we go
You're in my heart forever you know

I will not weep, I will not mourn you
I will laugh and applaud you
I will celebrate the life you lived
And I will live my life knowing you had so
much more to give

I will spread your message
I will teach what needs to be taught
I will give you the gift you wanted to give
I'll push for change
And you'll be the difference

I used to look twice at your fashion
But in me you spread passion
You were my guide, my best friend, my sister
Even when you found yourself a mister

In you I had my first friend
We are still in it together, this is not the end
You'll walk beside me my dear friend
Until the day we meet again

Your life was a festival full of song, life and
colour
You were unlike any other
Love always, your baby brother

Panic

Panic attacks really suck.

When your hands and body shake, and your body sweats inexcusably. Where your heart beats so fast, you think surely this is a heart attack. When you can have one billion thoughts racing through your head and none of them are helpful. When you feel all the things all at once, but none of them positive.

It can feel like you're trapped in a moment that you don't want to be in. Your thoughts take control and you beg them to let you go, even if it is just to take a second to breathe. But they've got a hold of you and they aren't letting you go anywhere but here.

Because this is what you deserve.

Try

Smile big, love wholeheartedly, laugh with joy and never ever feel alone. Every day will have its dawn, and you too can overcome this storm.

Be it patience, be it kindness, be it acceptance, be it pride. Be it loneliness, be it sadness, be it tears in your eyes. Know that it's truly okay that you feel this way inside. Know your worth, acknowledge your value and never give up, just try.

It's going to be okay soon, I promise you, just try.

On Your Way

You don't need all the answers.

You don't need to be surrounded by lots of people. You don't need to feel the highest of highs and the lowest of lows all the time.

All you need is to trust your mind, trust your heart and you will find that inner peace inside you.

I promise, you'll get there, you're already on your way.

Words

Words have impact.

I remember when I was younger constantly hearing the saying "sticks and stones may break my bones, but your words will never hurt me", and as a child it worked and I believed it.

But as I grew and learnt to be the man I am today, I learnt that our words, they have power. They can be used to bring joy, spread kindness and express love. But they can also hurt far more than any broken bone ever could or would.

They can cut like a knife and really stick with a person, sometimes even longer than the person who said them does.

Words are powerful things. Use them wisely.

Poison

Don't drink the poison just because you're thirsty.

Yes, things happened and went from good to bad to worse. But remember to always stay true to yourself, to your values and to what you believe in.

And then, I promise you, everything will work out the way you want it to.

Keep Going

You felt the same too familiar feelings, you weathered the storm, you did all you could until you couldn't anymore.

You chose to embrace the brightness of the sun, even if it meant enduring the rain. You chose to not give up, you were patient with yourself and you gave yourself time to heal. You stood tall, you overcame and you knew there would always be better days to come.

You chose to embrace the fear and despair instead of resisting it. You were kind to yourself and others. You spread love, acceptance and understanding, and you kept going.

Sometimes survival meant standing alone, sometimes it meant being surrounded by a sea of people, but no matter what, you kept going.

Be proud of how far you have come, and know that you can overcome anything and everything that comes your way.

Keep going, you're doing so well.

Let Go

Let go of what you cannot change. Let go of the painful memories. Let go of what doesn't add to your life or bring you joy.

Letting go doesn't have to be about giving up. It can be about giving yourself permission to heal your mind and your heart, and learning to breathe again.

To have hope again, to smile, to laugh and to love with your whole heart approaching the present and future with a sense of peace - yes you endured, but you came out the other side. Be proud of that, you have done so well.

Know that this doesn't have to be your life forever. Give yourself permission to go forth with love and kindness in your heart, ready for the next adventure.

No More

For the longest time I held onto this mentality that people always leave or die. I thought of it as this inevitable thing that would always happen and there was no point getting close to anyone. So I stopped putting myself out there out of fear of being vulnerable and told myself that if I was alone at least nobody could hurt me.

But the truth is that was only hurting myself. Truth is that it is an inevitable thing that we will all one day die and people will love and leave you along the way. But the journey you are on through life was never meant to be travelled on your own. It is a journey that should be shared, where memories are made, friends and love come and go and somewhere in amongst it all you create meaning out of your life.

I don't want to be alone anymore. I want to share in the love and joy that the world has to offer. I don't want to be scared anymore. I want to face whatever the present and the future has to offer with fearless abandon. If my past can teach me anything it's that I can confront anything that comes my way and I will be okay.

I want to laugh and I want to fall in love with people and with life again. Because I deserve that. I'm not giving up, not now and not ever again. I deserve to live my life to the fullest and I will.

I promise myself.

Friendship

For a long time I looked for friendships in all the wrong places.

I sought to find myself a feeling of belonging in London but I looked for it in all the wrong places, even when the warning signs and red flags were clear for all to see.

I tried to make things work even when I knew they couldn't, and didn't. I told myself it was my fault, that I was a bad person and a bad friend. That I could have, should have and would have done more to make whatever situation we were in better for the other person. That I was the person in the wrong and it was my fault every single time something went bad.

I told myself I needed more friends and was scared to be alone. I felt feelings of isolation and I really thought about going home.

I felt like I was the villain and to blame for anything that had gone wrong. I felt that I deserved nothing more than to be alone.

But there were some, a select few that stuck by me. That didn't give up on me, even when I was at my worst. They showed me kindness, offered me advice and reassurance, and were the only reminder at the time that I was not alone.

They wanted what was good for me and hated seeing me at my physical and mental worst. I told myself and them that I didn't deserve them but they still stuck by me anyway.

Even at my worst they still cared for and about me. And that's when I learnt that it didn't matter how many people I surrounded myself with. If I can just find myself some people that do genuinely care and want the best for me then I would never truly be alone.

And to those people, thank you for the laughter. Thank you for listening to me at my worst, through tears, pain and anxious thought patterns. Why? Because you helped me to turn my life around.

I learnt to see you as friends of quality, not of quantity. I learnt to trust your judgment and we stuck by each through the best and worst.

I learnt that I was never alone because I had friends that cared. You taught me what friendship really meant and I think maybe, just maybe, I've found friends for life.

Reckless Abandon

It's taken me some time to really acknowledge the reasons behind my fears of abandonment, and my ability to trust people again. You see, years ago I trusted someone, or rather they really trusted me. To a point where it created some really unhealthy boundaries. And while all I wanted was to be a good person and to ensure this person got the help they needed, I was too young and I lacked the expertise to really support this person. But despite all that, I wasn't going to just let this person feel as though they were alone.

I told myself I wasn't doing enough. They continued to hold on to the belief that I was the person that was going to get them out of the darkness, all while I wasn't acknowledging the darkness it was putting me in.

Of course I will always do my best to do good by the people around me, and I will do anything and everything I can to make sure a person never has to feel alone. But this experience engulfed me, it took away my spirit, my self belief and my trust in anyone, most of all in myself.

I was made aware that they had taken their life, something that unfortunately was a constant possibility in my time knowing them. Some months later, I learned that was all a lie. They were still living, and it was a result of my not having feelings for them. It was a horrifying experience to live through.

First of all, I have never held hate in my heart for anyone or anything. I truly wish this person well and have told them so. I'm glad they've gotten the help they needed, and the help that I could not give to them. But that feeling of having someone rely so heavily on me and like I not only let them down but I was in some way responsible for their passing - it took hold of me and never let me go.

So I chose to hide my pain for a really long time. It made me push away friends and any thoughts of romantic interest with anyone. Because if someone could do something like that to me, I felt surely I must be in some way the problem and something was wrong with me. I felt that people were better off without me, and that I was better off alone.

I was really hard on myself, I still am. And while I don't hold anything against this person, I am finally acknowledging how it made me feel. Worthless, humiliated, ashamed and a disappointment are words that weighed heavily on my mind for a long time. But not anymore.

I guess that's the thing about pain, it demands to be felt. You can choose to ignore it, you can bury it to the depths of your memory and try to move on - but acknowledging that pain and learning from it, that's a whole rollercoaster of emotions. It can hurt to come up, but once you work with that pain, you can enjoy the thrill of going down, letting go and moving forward with a sense of self worth and peace.

I have learnt that I am not my trauma. I am not the reason for the chaos, I'm not even part of the problem. I was just a kid doing my best in a crazy fucking world.

The other thing about pain, it stays with you - often longer than that person ever does. And so, I can confidently say I hold no angst or ill will towards this person. But the way it made me feel, the way I doubted everything about myself and questioned my worth, that stuck with me for a very long time.

All I'm saying is, don't bury your pain. It's uncomfortable, I know, to look it in the face and confront those wounds. But when you do, I guarantee you that you begin your journey towards peace, towards letting go and towards moving on.

Know that you are not your trauma, you're the brave warrior that looked fear in the face and said, you don't get to win, not today, not ever. And know that, just like the sun rises each day, so will you, and you will be okay again. I promise you that.

Change

One of the hardest lessons to learn is that we can't change the past. It seems kind of obvious that, but that doesn't stop the storm of regret, heartache and loss from hitting you hard.

It takes time but we learn that it's important to mourn for what's happened and what we have lost. But eventually after that storm, we do need to learn to look for and embrace the rainbow that follows. A rainbow full of joy, of self care, of love and acceptance.

Because it's important to accept what's happened, and to know that it doesn't have to define you. Your beating heart and unique mind weren't placed on this earth for you to suffer, but for you to thrive and succeed. And most importantly, to live the best life you can with the time that you do have.

We all have our demons, but please know that you are not defined by your flaws and past mistakes. You are defined by the person you choose to be. No you can't change the past but

when you learn to accept that, you also give
yourself permission to let go and move on.

When you learn to trust your own heart, your
own character and take confidence in the person
that you are, you learn that your opinion is the
only one that truly matters. It's important to have
good people around you, but you don't have to
put so much energy into others and their
opinions of you. You attract what you put out
into the world and the rest will follow. The
world has a way of making things right - trust
that it will.

So please give yourself permission to move
forward and take pride in the person you are and
have been. Let go and accept what has
happened, has happened - it's time to move on.

And I promise, when you do that you will find
that sense of freedom and peace you have been
searching for.

And it will be beautiful.

Unique

Know that nobody is going to do this for you.
You need to do it for yourself. You need to learn
to engage with what's standing in your way. You
need to learn to be okay with confronting what's
uncomfortable and make your own peace with it.

Nobody is going to save you but you can choose
to be there for yourself. You can choose to save
yourself and make your life what you always
dreamed of. You don't have to hide from it, you
don't have to run from it, but you do need to
look it in the eye and learn to be okay with it.

You need to be okay with the fact that not every
day is going to be a good one, but also learn to
look for the good in each day. You will learn to
be okay with fear and regret and loss and
goodbyes.

You will learn that it's okay to worry, to feel at a
loss, to cry - because it means it meant
something. But you will also learn that there's
beauty in being broken, because sometimes your

world does fall apart, but it also gives you the opportunity to piece it back together again.

If you really stick with it and try, you can also be lucky enough to learn from it. Know that you're not broken, you are far stronger than you know - please don't be afraid to believe in yourself, be kind to yourself and give yourself all the kindness and love that you deserve.

Know that there will never, ever be anyone quite like you. Thank you for bringing your inspiring mind and loving heart into this world, the world is better for it and always will be.

Purpose

The purpose of life is not to be happy.

If it was then I'd have failed at life more often than not. But none of us are or can be happy all the time.

I think the purpose of life is to be kind, to be giving of your time, knowledge and compassion. To share your stories of pain, trauma and devastation, but to emphasize your comeback story and the resilience you showed to bounce back and find peace when all felt lost.

It's about being brave, even when you feel everything but. It's about working hard at life, on yourself and feeling inner peace rather than external. It's about putting smiles on peoples faces, especially your own. It's about taking pride in who you are and the story you have to tell. Because yes maybe you weren't always happy, but you still stood tall and became the person you are today. Be proud of that.

And then maybe, when you're old, tired and grey you can look back on your life feeling as though you accomplished something truly special.

And when there comes the day for you to leave this earth, hopefully you can feel as though you're leaving it a better place as a result of you having lived in it.

Because no, you weren't always happy, but that was never the purpose. Your story, it's so beautiful already. Please go and keep filling the pages while you still can.

Sorry

I'm sorry your heart got broken into a million pieces.

I'm sorry that you lost the laughter in your life and everything seemed dark. I'm sorry that you pushed people away, not deliberately but out of fear and desperation. I'm sorry you lost sight of who you are and the person you've always been.

I promise you they are still inside of you.

I'm sorry that the light didn't shine on you when you needed it more than ever and you were left out in the cold all alone. I'm sorry that things got so dark that the anxiety and fear crept in like a thief in the night and never really went away - especially when you did everything you could to ask and want it to.

I'm sorry for how you were made to feel and how hard that was for you. I'm sorry for the questioning. I'm sorry for the lies. I'm sorry for the way that made you feel inside. I'm sorry for absolutely everything you've had to do. I'm sorry for the pain it caused and I'm sorry for how you still feel now, because even though it's over, your heart still hurts for what you went through.

I'm sorry that I expected so much of you and wanted more of you. That I wanted things to just be better without acknowledging the pain and hurt you felt inside. I'm sorry that this has sat with you and has always been by your side. I'm sorry that this happened to you and changed who you are.

But know that I'll always be proud of the character you have shown. The strength, and the courage it's taken to stand tall - especially when you're doing anything and everything not to fall. I'm proud of you in the daytime, and proud of you all night. Know that mistakes were made but it was never going to be perfect. Give yourself a break kid, your fire shines so bright.

I am so fucking proud of you.

Hey big sister,

This really should have been read out with us all surrounded by your family and friends, but as we know life had other plans.

Please know that I am forever grateful that I got to grow up with you as not only my big sister, but as my best friend. You were always looking out for me for as long as I can remember. You always saw the best in people and the fact that you believed in me meant more than I could have ever imagined growing up.

You had faith in me that I was going to be successful. That I would be a great teacher and we both dreamed of moving to London - and know that I'm here living it for the both of us. I often think about what it would be like to have you by my side living our dream together, but know that I feel you with me every single day. I might not see you, but I know you are guiding me forward, willing me through life. And know that I feel the same energy and passion you felt to make the world a better place through education, love and kindness.

You encouraged me to always dare to be different and to embrace that difference. You encouraged me even when I was in the wrong because you always saw the best in me and it meant the world to me, it still does. I am a better person having known and having called you my sister.

You amazed me growing up how you didn't care what people thought. You amazed me with your sense of fashion and how you always said what you were thinking, no matter how blunt it sounded. You amazed me with the outpouring of love for you when you first said goodbye. And you continue to amaze me every single day.

Your love, your warmth, your kindness and your big heart will always hold a special place inside me. There isn't a day that goes by where I don't think of you, miss you, but most of all that I'm not grateful that I get to call you my sister and friend. I love you now and always.

Happy 30th Birthday Big Sister

Goals Setting (Revisited)

Eight or so months ago I was in the worst place I honestly think I have ever been.

I felt lost, mentally and physically exhausted and trapped in a deep, dark hole of never-ending, gut wrenching pain. I didn't know what to do or what direction to take in life. All I knew was that I couldn't keep living my life feeling that way. But then something happened, something I truly believe saved my life. I was hurting but I didn't want to give up and so I started therapy.

And it was uncomfortable at first, to pour through the many reasons for my trauma. It was a dark existence that I doubted I'd ever get myself out of. But day by day, as I opened myself up more and more - I began to grow and get stronger. Don't get me wrong, I doubted that growth for a while because I still felt like my life was a mess. But I was finally sowing the seed for what was to come.

It wasn't comfortable, but it was never going to be. I had a lot of anxiety, of fear and a big lack of self confidence that I had to work through and I had to learn to adopt a positive growth mindset. Which is hard, especially when your head and heart are telling you that you are not good enough and are destined to nothing but to fail.

I learnt to listen to my inner child, and to champion my inner child. To speak to that little boy inside of me and to tell him that it was all going to be okay, that there is no need to fear and that all is not lost. I learnt that everything I have inside me is enough to overcome anything that is in front of me because I'd already done it. My life is a testament to that, for I have endured but I still got on with it and didn't give up. Trust me, there's strength and wisdom in recognising that.

I learnt to be more self aware and that I was the only person that could get myself out of that dark hole. But more than anything, I finally wanted to get myself out of it. No one wants to be unhappy, but sometimes facing up to the reasons for our unhappiness is a much scarier prospect than actually living with it every single day.

I began to believe in myself again. To believe that I too deserve to experience joy, success, to laugh, to fall in love. I learnt that the pain, the heartbreak and the agony of loss was all part of the human experience but it didn't have to forever define me. I learnt to fall in love with life again.

I learnt to surround myself with good people. To take risks again without fear of the fallout or of being abandoned. I was honest with myself and that helped me to be more honest with others. I learnt to let go of my past and to recognise that while people do sometimes leave, and they die, that that's no reason to destine yourself to being alone. Yes people will leave, but we will all one day. That's no reason to not enjoy the time we do have.

I've still got some way to go on my journey, but I am so proud of how far I have come. I know that it doesn't just come with going to therapy, that I need to do the work and it's a constant throughout your life. But it's so nice to feel a sense of achievement, of growth, and most importantly, of peace.

And it's so exciting to be falling in love with life again.

Letter

Hey Big Sister,

I've really been wanting to talk to you about something recently. Remember way back when we talked about me and love? How you told me that I deserve to find someone who is going to make me laugh, care about me, and most importantly, want me for me, and not some other version of myself - well I found her, and I know you'd really like her.

I have been so terrified to put myself out there for such a long time. The idea of trusting someone, of being intimate with another person - well it terrified me, but you already know that. I also know that you've been there giving me signs along the way.

Ever since you left us, I still notice the signs that you're around. Anytime I've really needed you, I've only had to look for the rainbows and in your music to know that while you're not at arm's reach, you are still around and with me every day.

Ever since the first evening I met her, I have
noticed the ladybugs. Something since you
passed that I can't explain. But just like the
rainbows and music, when I've needed you I
often spot a ladybug and it brings me comfort. I
have seen so many ladybugs around lately and I
know it probably makes no sense, but I like to
see it as you giving me a sign that I've found
someone really good for me and that you
approve, that you're happy for me. But maybe
that's just me clutching at something that isn't
there.

Big sister, she makes the bad days easier just by
her smile. She makes me believe that there is
some good in me. I know I can trust her with my
whole heart and not have to hide my
vulnerabilities from her. And yes, the thought of
me finding and meeting someone who I can
open up with and really trust, would have been
something I'd have believed impossible once
upon a time but she makes it so easy every
single day.

I feel my anxiety and my trauma get smaller
whenever I am with her. She makes me see that
anything I've ever done and do is good enough,

and that I am good enough. She makes me feel like I can conquer the whole world and anything that comes in my way because I have her by my side. She makes me feel like I deserve to laugh, to smile, to be happy. She makes falling more and more in love with her so easy every single day.

I just wanted to say thank you. I know trusting someone and being vulnerable with someone was always going to be hard, because, well the last person I trusted like that was… you. But what I am remembering more and more every day is how much you believed in me and wanted good for me, how you wanted this for me. You still make me a better person every single day.

Thank you for being the best friend I could have ever asked for and for teaching me what it really means to love someone.

I love you, and I miss you big sister

Tame The Beast

It's taken me a long time to really comprehend how much this year has effected me and I don't think I did until I really invested myself in therapy.

Facing uncomfortable truths and facing your demons head on meant going within and opening up long closed doors.

I don't think I understood what a relationship really felt like until I met her. To feel at peace in their company, to have open communication and to have genuine care for each other. I didn't think that existed.

I recognised that my past experiences have made me feel so used to things turning bad or having to feel so on edge with my anxiety that the only option I feel like I've got is to run. But then I never do out of fear and decide it's better to be in an unhealthy relationship than to be alone with my thoughts. Because there was nothing worse than that.

I don't think I understood what peace was until I finally felt it. Not just at peace with a situation or a relationship ending, but actual true inner peace. I craved it for so long that I didn't think it was possible.

Because it was the impossible for a really long time. It was something I wouldn't dare to confront or fight for, and it was never time to poke and wake the beast.

But what I learnt is to embrace the fear. To confront every fear and every insecurity. To talk and to cry and panic and feel painful anxiety. I learnt to poke and wake the beast within.

I had to face it. There were no two ways around that. I had been putting it off for my entire life and I was never, ever happy because of it.

This year has long felt like the worst year of my life. I really went to some really dark places and I highly doubted that I'd ever get myself out of them. I lost my way because it felt like there was no way to go. I was lost physically and mentally and felt I had no real purpose or value.

But I learnt to face the beast with determination, resilience and grace. I learnt to listen to his anger and pain and I learnt to care for him. Because he had hurt me, but he also was me.

I learnt to shower him with care, kindness and love. I gave him permission to speak his truth and told him I believed in him, even when no one else did. I got him to stand tall and be proud of his journey of struggle, strength and resilience.

I learnt to forgive him for what he had done and told him that he was good enough. That he deserved to be happy. To laugh. To love.

And somewhere along there in amongst it all, this year also became the best year of my life. I had finally confronted the beast and learnt to see him as a guide and a friend.

I learnt to be comfortable being uncomfortable. I learnt that I could overcome anything from my past that haunted me because I already had, I was living proof of that. It was over and I had won.

I learnt that I deserve to feel genuinely and authentically happy. That I deserve to surround myself with good people who genuinely care for me. And that I deserve to fall in love with someone that really takes my breath away.

I learnt to focus on the things I can control and spent less time worrying about the things I can't. I learnt that I didn't have to let the darkness consume me and that there was beauty from within.

I learnt to fall in love with life again.